The
North
American
Indians

Inuit

The

Titles in the North American Indians series include:

The North American Indians

The
Inuit

Charles and Linda George

KIDHAVEN PRESS
An imprint of Thomson Gale, a part of The Thomson Corporation

Detroit • New York • San Francisco • San Diego • New Haven, Conn.
Waterville, Maine • London • Munich

LIBRARY OF CONGRESS CATALOGING-IN-PUBLICATION DATA

George, Charles, 1949–
    The Inuit / by Charles and Linda George.
        p. cm. — (North American Indians)
    Includes bibliographical references and index.
    ISBN 0-7377-2626-1 (hard cover : alk. paper)
    1. Inuit—Nunavut—History—Juvenile literature. 2. Inuit—Nunavut—Social life and customs—Juvenile literature. I. George, Linda. II. Title. III. Series.
    E99.E7G333 2005
    971.9'50049712—dc22

                                                                                    2004019198

Printed in the United States of America

Contents

Chapter One

The Land and the People

The Inuit, people who have inhabited the far northern regions of North America for at least three thousand years, have also been called Eskimos. This name, meaning "eaters of raw meat," came from the Cree Indians of east-central Canada. Though the term accurately describes them, the Inuit consider the name Eskimo an insult. Inuit means "the people" or "the real people" in their language, Inuktitut. A single individual is called Inuk, which means "person."

Origins of the Inuit

The Inuit, although considered Native Americans, are more closely related physically and genetically to Asians than to American Indians. The ancestors of American Indians arrived on the continent of North America at least twelve thousand years ago, crossing a land bridge from Asia. Ancestors of the Inuit probably arrived along the coast of the Alaskan Peninsula by boat much later, only five thousand to eight thousand years ago.

Early Inuit depended almost entirely on the sea for food, clothing, and shelter. They came to North America in search of sea mammals such as whales and seals, followed them north and east along the coast of the Arctic Ocean, and eventually settled in areas that became Alaska, Canada, and Greenland. This migration from the Alaskan Peninsula began around four thousand years ago. Today, forty-one thousand Inuit make up the most widespread native population in the world. Their lands

Today, the Inuit inhabit regions of Alaska, Canada, Greenland, and Russia. Pictured here are Inuit villagers in Alaska.

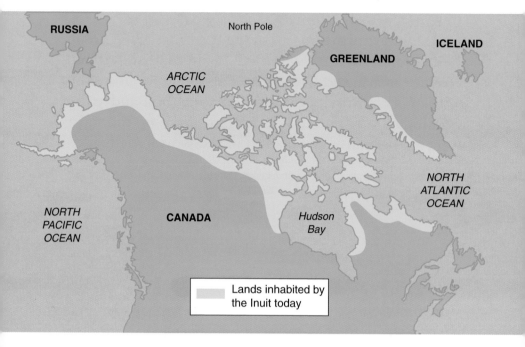

extend 3,000 miles (4,827km) from the Aleutian Islands and the tip of Siberia in the west to Greenland in the east.

How We Know About the Early Inuit

The early Inuit lived in one of the Earth's most remote regions. They also never developed a written language. For these reasons, it is difficult for scientists to learn about how the early Inuit lived. Archaeologists (scientists who study ancient cultures) can piece together information about them by examining items they find at old Inuit campsites. These items include tools, evidence of foods the Inuit ate, and so forth.

Another way archaeologists learn about the early Inuit is by listening to stories passed down by word of mouth for generations within modern Inuit families. These stories can tell scientists about lifestyles, folklore, religious beliefs, and customs of the ancestors of today's Inuit.

Finally, scientists can read what European explorers wrote about their meetings with groups of Inuit during the early twentieth century. Between 1900 and 1940, adventurers such as Knud Rasmussen, Peter Freuchen, and Gontran de Poncins traveled to the Arctic. There, they found Inuit who lived much as their ancestors had lived. The journals of these explorers are rich with details about how those Inuit lived and how their environment affected their lives.

Land of the Midnight Sun

In arctic regions of North America, there are three types of terrain—the **ice cap**, rocky coasts, and **tundra**. Ice caps are areas of land covered year-round with ice and snow. Since the polar ice cap never thaws, few people live there. The early Inuit traveled there only on hunting trips. Farther south, in the southern Arctic Ocean, ice

An Inuit man gliding along the Alaskan coast in a kayak uses a spear to hunt fish.

up to three feet thick forms in the winter, but waterways are open for the brief summer season, which allowed early Inuit hunters to follow whale herds.

Rocky coasts lining the southern Arctic Ocean also freeze completely in winter, making fishing difficult. During those months, the Inuit hunted polar bears and seals. In summer, the coasts thaw, allowing the Inuit to fish. Only small plants called lichens can live along the rocky coasts. They are not edible, nor can they provide fuel for campfires.

Inland, vast rolling plains called tundra produce some vegetation in summer, but its use is limited. Tundra is a low, flat, treeless region covered with heath, mosses, grasses, and shrubs. The Inuit used some of this plant material as fuel for campfires, but mostly to stuff inside their clothing as insulation. Although the plants on the tundra provide grazing for animals, they do not yield any food for humans.

This region annually receives up to 20 inches (50.8cm) of rain. This is enough to support low-growing plants that are eaten by caribou, musk oxen, small mammals, and seabirds. Some inland groups of Inuit hunted these animals, but most were coast dwellers, living primarily on sea mammals and fish.

During the arctic winter, the sun disappears for a long polar night lasting weeks or even months, depending on **latitude**. This is because the axis of the Earth leans away from the Sun during winter. During the brief summer, when the Earth leans toward the Sun, the Sun sometimes shines twenty-four hours a day. Because of this, the Arctic is nicknamed "Land of the Midnight Sun."

Even with that much sunshine, summer temperatures seldom rise above 50 degrees Fahrenheit (10°C). In winter, temperatures can drop to –50 degrees (–45°C). Living under such conditions is difficult. As in any harsh climate, lifestyle adaptations are required for survival.

A young Inuit boy drags home a large block of ice to melt for drinking water.

Living in the Arctic

Over the centuries, the Inuit have adapted to the cold, barren climate of the Arctic. This has allowed them to live in a region of the world most people consider uninhabitable. The diet of the early Inuit consisted of raw fish, boiled seal meat, and **blubber**. Such high levels of fat in their diet provided much-needed body heat. This helped their bodies withstand the intense cold.

11

The Inuit also helped ensure their survival by banding together into small, tightly knit groups. These groups usually included members of the same extended family—adult brothers and sisters and their families, grandparents, aunts, uncles, and so on. Family groups contained between twelve and fifty people. Individual family units within the extended family group normally built their homes near each other, forming small settlements. Each group was led by the eldest male still able to hunt. This man, the umialik, or boss, led family discussions and helped resolve conflicts.

An Inuit family shares a meal in their igloo. Traditional Inuit families were small and very tightly knit.

Living in isolation in such tightly knit family groups sometimes led to conflict between family members. These were often resolved by wrestling matches or song duels. In a song duel, the angry parties made up insulting songs about each other. Other members of the family, or sometimes the umialik, decided the winner. Sometimes the loser was driven from the community.

Each settlement used one person's house as a gathering place, or qargi, where people met for conversation and ritual. Different family groups seldom banded together except when hunting large game, such as whale, walrus, polar bear, and **caribou**.

Chapter Two

Daily Life in the Arctic

Many people, when they think of the Inuit, picture people wearing sealskin clothing and living in igloos on the polar ice cap. They imagine people driving dogsleds across ice and snow to hunt seal, caribou, and polar bear, or paddling **kayaks** onto the ocean to hunt whales. This does not describe the lifestyle of all Inuit, but is fairly accurate for the early Inuit, at least for part of the year.

The Hunt

Early Inuit were skilled hunters who had vast knowledge about animal behavior and climate. They knew the habits of every land and sea animal inhabiting the Arctic. They studied sea ice—its appearance and the sound it made when stepped on—for signs warning them of danger. They learned to navigate in the thickest fog and through the darkest nights by sensing ocean currents beneath their skin-covered boats.

In their boats, either two-man kayaks or large, open boats called **umiaks**, the Inuit hunted whales and other sea mammals with toggle-headed **harpoons**, an Inuit invention. They separated on contact, allowing the handle to come free, but leaving the point and its harpoon line attached to the animal. This allowed the Inuit to pull the animal out of the water, or at least forced the animal to pull against the hunters and weaken itself, so it could be caught more easily.

On land, Inuit hunters had to sneak up on their prey to get close enough to use spears. They usually wrapped themselves in polar bear skins so they would blend in with the snow. When they were close enough, they thrust their spears into the animal.

Dogsleds

When hunting on land, the Inuit used dogsleds to follow their prey and to carry the game back to camp. Sleds were made of whatever materials were on hand—either wood or whalebone—with two parallel runners covered with ivory or caribou antler. Some Inuit even used frozen fish wrapped in sealskin as runners!

An Inuit hunter in Greenland drives his sled dogs across a frozen sea as he searches for seals, walruses, and polar bears.

Sled dogs, ideally suited to the harsh climate, had bushy tails and coats up to four inches thick. The Inuit considered their dogs partners, not pets. In spring, when the ice formed sharp crystals, some Inuit put sealskin boots on their dogs' feet to protect their paws. Because dogsleds provided the only form of transportation over the ice, a good team of dogs was critical to an Inuk's survival.

The typical dog team consisted of seven or eight dogs harnessed in a fan-shaped formation. This allowed their weight to be spread out on the ice. Drivers controlled their teams with whistles and other sounds, along with whips made from seal or walrus hide.

Bounty of the Sea and Land

The Inuit used dogsleds not only to hunt on land, but also to move camp to the edge of the Arctic Ocean to hunt for whales. The primary source of food for many early Inuit was the bowhead whale. Herds of these 60-ton giants (54.4 metric tons) migrated each year to the edge of the polar ice cap. The bowhead provided the Inuit with large amounts of meat and blubber. Whales also provided **baleen**, a tough, flexible material the Inuit used to make fishing lines, nets, and other equipment. Whalebones served as the framework for boats, sleds, storage racks, grave markers, and homes.

The Inuit also hunted caribou, musk oxen, seals, walruses, and polar bears for meat. They used the skins to make clothes, boats, and summer tents. They hunted small-

Inuit hunters drag a walrus back to their village. The Inuit depended on several marine and land animals for survival.

er animals, too, such as sea otters, rabbits, and foxes. The Inuit crafted tools from bones, antlers, teeth, and horns. Tendons were used as thread and harpoon lines. Small bones became finer tools such as leather punches.

One of the most important tools of the Inuit was the needle, also made from small bones. When the Inuit were traveling, having a needle often meant the difference between life and death. If an Inuk's torn clothing could not be mended, he or she might freeze to death.

Inuit Clothing

Inuit men and women typically wore clothing made from animal skins, mostly caribou, seal, and polar bear. Women sewed skins together with the twisted **sinew** of beluga whales or caribou. The best skins came from cari-

In this photo from the early 1900s, an Inuit mother dressed in caribou skin poses with her child.

bou killed in the fall, when their coats were thick for the coming winter.

In winter, the Inuit wore two sets of clothing—an inner garment with the fur turned inward against the body, and an outer garment with the fur facing outward. Most wore a parka with a fur-lined hood as the outer garment. Water-resistant mittens and boots of sealskin or caribou skin protected hands and feet. Dry grass, down from water birds, or moss provided extra insulation and helped absorb moisture inside mittens and boots.

In summer, the Inuit wore lighter garments made from lighter skins such as seal. Many times, they wore only what had been their inner winter garments, with the fur turned outward.

Arctic Homes

Inuit homes, like Inuit clothing, were perfectly adapted to the Arctic. The Inuit used three types of homes— igloos (called iglus in Inuktitut), sod houses called qarmaqs, and, in summer, skin-covered tents called tupiqs. They used iglus, or "snow houses," only as temporary shelters on hunting trips. These houses were built of blocks of snow piled into a dome shape, with a tunnel entrance to keep out the cold.

Most Inuit lived year-round, except during hunting trips and during summer, in half-buried sod houses with frameworks of driftwood or whalebone. Layers of rock, soil, and animal skins insulated these one-room homes. They were cozy enough to allow Inuit to wear few clothes inside, warmed by a small oil lamp and their own body heat. The room was round, generally 15 feet (4.6m) across and 8 feet (2.4m) high, large enough to sleep eight to twelve people. Entrances were narrow tunnels dug deeper than the level of the main room to allow fresh air to enter without letting in cold winds.

During the summer, Inuit families lived in tents covered with sealskin like this one.

Sometimes, the Inuit stored food, clothing, and hunting gear in nooks near the entrance. During blizzards, sled dogs slept in a separate area in the entry tunnel. Most homes had no furniture other than a raised platform for sleeping. Roofs had a small hole to allow smoke from lamps and small cooking fires to exit. Some had skylights made from seal intestines. These panels allowed light inside during the day, and at night, light from oil lamps burning inside glowed through them to guide hunters home.

Men's and Women's Work

As in many early societies, early Inuit men and women had separate tasks. An Inuit man's primary duties were to hunt, to build homes, and to prepare a cache (a store-house for meat). Men also made weapons, boats, and sleds.

Most of the year, Inuit women stayed home to care for children, cook, and keep the home warm. They also cut and tanned skins, made thread, and sewed the family's clothing. During summer, they gathered grass to use as insulation in winter clothing. Some Inuit women set traps for small animals and birds. They were almost never allowed to hunt for large game. Inuit folklore suggested that animals would be offended if a woman hunted caribou, bear, or whale, and might go away. Wives did go on the hunt with their husbands, but only to process meat and hides after kills were made.

An Inuit woman hangs whale meat to dry. Women were responsible for processing meat after the hunt.

Leisure Time

Because of the harsh climate in which they lived, both Inuit men and women spent most of their time working. Little time was left for leisure. The only pastime common among the Inuit was storytelling. The Inuit loved telling stories for fun, entertainment, and as a means of passing history from generation to generation. Storytellers sometimes used complicated string figures to illustrate their stories.

Traditional stories demonstrated how people and nature could live together peacefully. They also contained lessons for children about how to behave. They taught that it was important to be truthful, patient, generous, and calm. Stories also taught children to respect old customs. Inuit stories included events from the family's past, but also myths and legends associated with the spirit world.

Chapter Three

The Spirit World

The early Inuit lived at the mercy of forces of nature they did not fully understand—wind, water, snow, and ice. They did not fully understand the cycle of birth and death, or what the sun, moon, or stars were. Like many early cultures, they told fables, legends, and myths to explain the world around them.

Because they believed in spirits, they were careful not to break **taboos**, rules that forbid certain activities because they are thought to bring harm. For protection, they carried **amulets**—objects they believed held magical powers. Also, because they faced so many dangers in nature, they had **shamans**, or medicine men, with power over nature, who could contact the spirit world.

Animism

Everything in early Inuit life revolved around traditional behavior, rituals, and **animism**—a belief that spirits inhabit all things. The Inuit believed all people, animals, forces of nature, and objects had spirits, called inuas.

Since life revolved around the hunt, many rituals involved animals the Inuit hunted. They believed animals had spirits that could think, feel, and talk. The Inuit believed animals would give themselves to hunters who acted properly toward them. They performed rituals before a hunt to show respect for their prey and to give thanks to the animals' spirits.

After killing a whale, seal, or walrus, the Inuit trickled melted snow into its mouth to help it on its way to the spirit world. They believed that since these animals lived in salt water, they were eternally thirsty. The Inuit performed a similar ceremony after a caribou hunt. Since this land mammal ate only plants, hunters believed it craved fat. To thank a slain animal for allowing itself to be killed, the Inuit rubbed whale or seal blubber on its nose.

Inuit hunters strip the meat from a pair of caribou after giving thanks to the spirit of the animals.

Taking care to obey taboos associated with animal spirits, an Inuit woman uses her teeth to soften a caribou hide.

The Inuit believed the spirits of whales remained on land after their deaths to observe human behavior. Eventually, these spirits returned to the sea to report what they had learned to other whales. If the whale spirit saw humans showing the proper respect, whales would return the following spring and allow themselves to be caught. If they observed disrespectful behavior, they would stay away, and people might starve.

Taboos and Rituals

To avoid offending animal spirits, the Inuit obeyed taboos associated with the hunt. They believed land animals and sea animals should never be mixed. The Inuit never ate meat from both sea and land animals at the same meal. Caribou was never cooked over a driftwood fire, because driftwood came from the sea. A knife used to butcher a whale must be tied with sealskin, not caribou sinew. Women never sewed caribou skins while living on sea ice.

Other taboos and rituals involved the Inuit concept of the soul. When a caribou was slaughtered, its ears were not cut off until the butchering was finished, to keep its soul from turning into an evil spirit. When a seal was killed, its bladder was saved. The Inuit believed the soul of the seal lived in the bladder. Once a year, they threw the bladders into the sea, returning them to other seals so they could be reborn, and so the next hunting season would be a good one.

Gods and Goddesses

The Inuit believed everything in nature had a spirit, but certain elements—the ocean and the sky—were especially powerful. Chief among the Inuit gods and goddesses was a sea goddess known as Sedna, the "Old Woman of the Sea." She ruled over lesser spirits. Many Inuit considered her the mother of land and sea creatures and the provider of life.

Another important **deity** was Sila, the spirit who resided in the air, controlling weather. Most Inuit feared this god because of the power weather had to inflict hardship and death.

Heaven and Hell

Despite their harsh environment, most Inuit were casual about death. To them, there was little to fear. Arctic life was difficult, so they focused more on life than on what comes after death.

The Inuit concept of heaven and hell varied from place to place in the Arctic. Most agreed there were two lands of the dead, one pleasant and one unpleasant. In a climate where being snug and comfortable usually meant digging into the Earth for shelter, Inuit heaven was below the Earth. Heaven had abundant game to hunt, and friends and relatives who had gone before were there. The unpleasant place, the equivalent of hell, was in the sky, associated with starvation and cold.

The Human Spirit

The Inuit believed humans have more than a single spirit. Each person has many parts—a body, a soul, a name, a personality, and breath. Each has a life of its own.

According to Inuit tradition, a person's name had mystical power. Some Inuit never said their own names aloud for fear of breaking the magic. When a person died, his or her name could be given to a newborn child, bringing

Traditional Inuit belief held that the spirits of deceased family members could inhabit the bodies of children.

with it magic to protect the child. Once given the name, a baby was expected to have the personality and traits of the relative. Relatives might call a child "mother," "grandfather," or "aunt" because they believed the baby had the soul of the dead loved one.

Rituals associated with the naming of a baby were carefully followed, to avoid offending the spirit of the recently departed. The name of a person who had died was never spoken until a newborn received it, and a child was never called by name until the naming ceremony.

The Role of the Shaman

The Inuit believed some men and women possessed magical powers. These people were angakoks, or shamans. According to Inuit tradition, shamans could shake the Earth, transform themselves into animals, walk on clouds, make themselves invisible, and raise the dead. Early Inuit believed shamans regularly flew away to visit the gods, to retrieve lost souls, and to gain information about the future.

A woodcarving shows a shaman performing a seance. The Inuit believed shamans wielded terrific magical powers.

Shamans carved amulets like this wooden walrus to help them commune with the spirit world.

In addition to these mystical duties, shamans also served as medicine men, healing the sick with magic. The Inuit believed evil spirits caused illnesses, and to cure them, the shaman drove out the spirits.

Amulets

To aid them in communing with the spirit world, shamans crafted amulets, small statues of men or animals thought to carry magical powers. Angoaks, or "sacred charms," were usually carved from wood, ivory, bone, or antler. Inuit men believed carving images of the animals they hunted made them better hunters.

Other objects taken from animals or birds—teeth, feet, skin, noses, or claws—could also be amulets. Ravens, for example, were considered clever and hardy birds. To tap into the bird's spiritual power, parents hung the foot of a raven around the neck of a newborn baby. They felt it would protect the baby during its first dangerous days.

Each amulet had its own power—to steady a hunter's hand when throwing a harpoon or to prevent a head-ache, for example. Individuals sometimes owned many of them. Most people sewed amulets onto their clothing or wore them dangling from a special belt.

29

Chapter Four

The Road to Nunavut

The traditional way of life has ended for most Inuit. Today, most live in wooden houses instead of tents or sod houses. In place of animal skins, most wear modern clothing. They speak English, Danish, or Russian in addition to Inuktitut. They hunt from snowmobiles and motorboats rather than dogsleds, kayaks, and umiaks. Rifles have replaced spears and bows and arrows. Today, few Inuit live in isolation. They receive satellite television programming and have access to the Internet. Modern Inuit, unlike their ancestors, compete in the economic world, not the world of nature.

Outsiders Bring Change

Less than one hundred years ago, many Inuit in remote regions of north-central Canada lived much as their ancestors had lived. For others, change began much earlier. Beginning in the 1600s, several factors affected the lifestyle of the early Inuit. Some American Indian tribes, pushed northward by the arrival of European explorers, trappers, and settlers, hunted the Inuit's caribou.

The second change came when European and American whalers arrived, hunting bowhead whales for oil and baleen. Fewer whales brought further hardship. With the loss of caribou and whale, many Inuit became dependent upon handouts from Europeans and Americans.

Explorers and whalers traded with Inuit groups they encountered, bringing guns, cloth, metal, tools, and musical instruments. These items improved the lives of the Inuit. But traders also brought alcohol and tobacco, which did not improve their lives. Outsiders also brought diseases—measles, tuberculosis, influenza, diphtheria, and polio—against which the Inuit had no defense.

Inuit villagers greet nineteenth-century European explorers. The arrival of Europeans forever changed traditional Inuit life.

In the late 1700s, a fourth major change came. Catholic and Anglican missionaries arrived and established schools and churches to educate and convert the Inuit. By 1800 almost all Inuit had converted to Christianity.

Further Changes

In the early twentieth century, the Inuit began trading furs to support themselves. However, the 1930s brought a decline in the fur trade, causing the Inuit economic hardship and increased dependence on government assistance. The establishment of five government-sponsored residential schools further disrupted Inuit culture. The Canadian government required Inuit children as young as five to leave their families for months or years at a time to attend these schools.

In this photo from 1937, an Inuit family gathers around a record player to listen to music.

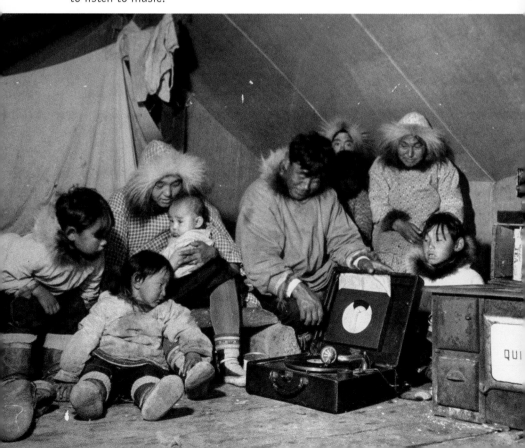

During the 1940s and 1950s, contact between the Inuit and the modern world increased significantly due to World War II and its aftermath. From 1941 to 1945, the U.S. Air Force built air bases in the Arctic to resupply war aircraft and ships headed for Europe. These bases brought thousands of non-Inuit people to the Arctic. After the war ended, the United States built radar installations and missile bases in the Arctic that brought even more outsiders.

During the same years, the Canadian government forced Inuit families to leave their native lands and relocate into settlements in Manitoba and the Northwest Territories. Conditions for the Inuit reached a low point in the 1950s. A 1958 study showed that one in eight Canadian Inuit suffered from tuberculosis. More than one-quarter of all babies died before the age of one, and the average Inuk could expect to live only to the age of twenty-five. Rates of suicide, alcoholism, and family violence were higher than national averages. Unemployment was also high.

Beginning in the late 1960s and early 1970s, native organizations formed to discuss Inuit problems and seek solutions. They pursued land claims against the Canadian and American governments to recover some of their native lands.

Nunavut

For Canadian Inuit, 1973 marked a turning point. In that year, three Canadian Supreme Court rulings supported their land claims, and the Canadian government agreed to negotiations. Over the next twenty years, talks between Canadian Inuit and the Canadian government continued.

In 1993 the Canadian parliament passed the Nunavut Land Claims Agreement Act, the largest land settlement in Canadian history. Canada agreed to pay the Inuit more

Inuit boys display the Nunavut flag in April 1999 during a ceremony to mark the creation of the territory of Nunavut.

than $1 billion between 1993 and 2007. It also gave legal title to more than 700,000 square miles (1,813,000sq km) to the Inuit. This led the way for passage of the Nunavut Act, which officially created a new territory from part of the Northwest Territories of northern Canada.

On April 1, 1999, the territory of Nunavut became a reality. Nunavut, meaning "our land" in Inuktitut, is Canada's largest territory, making up almost 20 percent of the nation's land area. Eighty-five percent of its twenty-seven thousand citizens are Inuit. Its capital and largest community (with five thousand inhabitants) is Iqaluit, which means "the place where the fish are." Formerly known as Frobisher Bay, Iqaluit is located on the southern coast of Baffin Island.

The creation of Nunavut is a matter of pride for the Inuit. They consider it a major step toward preserving their heritage and their culture. However, there is still much to be done.

Looking to the Future, and to the Past

The Inuit have always been able to adapt to changes in their environment. Outside influence took once self-reliant hunters living on the Arctic ice to the brink of destruction as a people. Many lost hope and had to rely on government assistance. They were forced to allow

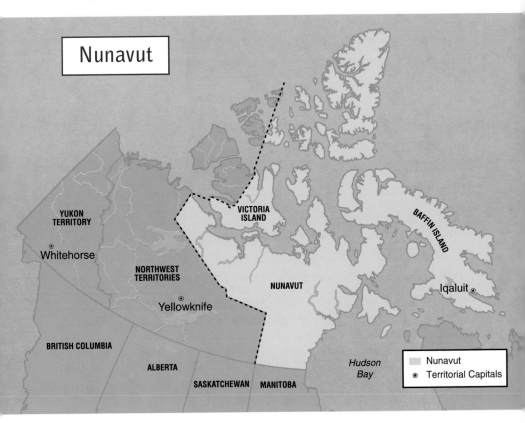

the Canadian government to decide where they lived, what they ate, how their children were raised, and even what language they spoke. Today, a younger generation is leading the Inuit toward a renewed awareness of their ancient culture.

In four generations, the Inuit went from seminomadic hunters to the Internet age. They are determined to tackle the challenges of the modern world head-on, while preserving two elements traditionally central to their culture—the family unit and ties to the land.

Today, as in the days of the early Inuit, family is the foundation of Inuit culture. Inuit families are large and interconnected, with support from the rest of the community and the region. Despite the arrival in the 1970s and 1980s of satellite television and radio signals, bringing world events and popular fads and fashions to the Arctic, native traditions are still important. In spite of VCRs, video games, the Internet, movie theaters, and fast food, thousands of years of tradition still shape the nature of Inuit communities.

Optimistic About the Future

Hunting is still one of the most important elements of Inuit culture. Although store-bought food is readily available, most Inuit still rely heavily upon the game they hunt and the fish they catch, just as their ancestors did hundreds of years ago. Modern Inuit still cherish their youth and their elders. Elders in Inuit society bring wisdom and knowledge of the traditional ways of the Inuit. They have kept Inuit traditions alive for younger generations.

Most Inuit today live in established communities, but many leave these settlements during the spring and summer to set up camps. They get away from modern

A woman in Nunavut walks past a stop sign marked in both English and Inuktitut.

distractions for a while to immerse their children in their language and culture. Splitting time between the modern world and the world of their ancestors allows them to restore their culture while still facing the challenges of the future.

The people of Nunavut, along with all Inuit in Canada, Alaska, and Greenland, face problems. Among them are

Inuit elders continue to work to keep traditional Inuit practices alive for future generations.

sparse resources, distant markets, a harsh climate, and a population not as well prepared for modern commerce as many in today's global economy. However, today's Inuit are optimistic about the future, just as their ancestors must have been, following whale herds to a new world.

Glossary

amulets: Objects, either natural or man-made (such as carvings or pieces of jewelry), that are thought to possess magical power to protect their owners from harm.

animism: The belief that animals, plants, inanimate objects, and natural phenomena, such as wind, fire, and water, have souls.

baleen: A fernlike growth in the mouths of whales that strains small animals called plankton from seawater.

blubber: The fat under the skin of a whale or seal.

caribou: A large North American mammal of the deer family, related to reindeer.

deity: A god or goddess.

harpoons: Long spears with an attached rope that can be thrown or shot out of a special gun, usually used for hunting large fish or whales.

ice cap: A mound of ice that covers an area of land and gets bigger as snow falls, melts, and then freezes.

kayaks: Narrow covered boats in which the rider sits and moves through the water by paddling.

latitude: The position of a place, measured in degrees north or south of the equator.

shamans: People thought to have special powers to communicate with and influence the spirit world, to guide souls, cure illnesses, and so on.

sinew: A strong fiber or band of tissue that connects a muscle to a bone; a tendon.

taboos: Activities or statements that are forbidden.

tundra: A cold area of northern North America, Europe, and Asia where there are no trees and the soil under the surface of the ground is permanently frozen.

umiaks: Large, open boats made of wood or whale bones and animal hides, propelled by paddling.

For Further Exploration

Books

Brian and Cherry Alexander, *What Do We Know About the Inuit?* New York: Peter Bedrick Books, 1995. Appealing and easy to read for young readers, this richly illustrated book has been called one of the best introductions to Inuit culture for children.

Raymond Bial, *Inuit.* New York: Benchmark Books, 2002. Fact packed and full of historical and contemporary photos, this book focuses on spiritual beliefs, family values, traditions, art forms, and recipes. One chapter is devoted to Inuit language, with a pronunciation guide. Written in clear, respectful language, this book may be a bit advanced for very young readers.

Danielle Corriveau, *Inuit of Canada.* Minneapolis, MN: Lerner, 2002. The story of past and present Inuit, emphasizing their use of natural resources. Well designed, with short sections for easier understanding. Includes large, full-color photos and attractive layouts.

Jennifer Fleischner, *The Inuits: People of the Arctic.* Brookfield, CT: Millbrook Press, 1995. This book focuses on the Inuit of Alaska, with chapters on survival in the harsh climate of the Arctic, passing on of traditions and values, the influence of explorers, and the life of the Inuit today.

Barbara A. Gray-Kanatiiosh, *Inuit.* Edina, MN: ABDO Publishing, 2002. A brief overview of the Inuit's homeland, with chapters on society, homes, food, clothing, crafts, family, myths, and the effects, both good and bad, of contact with Europeans. Includes a short biographical sketch of an Inuit singer-songwriter.

Rachel A. Koestler-Grack, *The Inuit: Ivory Carvers of the Far North.* Mankato, MN: Blue Earth Books, 2004. This book focuses on ivory carving, and includes a recipe for blueberry-topped snowcream and instructions for carving soap animals and playing Inuit games. Includes eye-catching graphics and sidebars.

Allison Lassieur, *The Inuit.* Mankato, MN: Bridgestone Books, 2000. Written in consultation with a cultural specialist, this book features maps and "Fast Facts" about such topics as Inuit homes, clothing, food, language, religion, families, and carving. Includes color photos.

Andrew Santella, *The Inuit.* New York: Childrens, 2001. An easy reader that includes plenty of scientific and cultural facts.

Suzanne M. Williams, *The Inuit.* New York: Franklin Watts, 2003. A look at the history and culture of the Inuit, focusing on traditions and customs as well as contemporary life. Includes good-quality photos and links to authoritative Web sites.

Caryn Yacowitz, *Inuit Indians.* Chicago: Heinemann Library, 2003. This book provides basic information about sled dogs, igloos, Inuit sun goggles, how they hunt seals, and how they use string figures to tell stories.

Web Sites
Government of Nunavut (www.gov.nu.ca). The official Web site of the territory of Nunavut.

Indigenous People, Canadian Arctic Profile (http://collections.ic.gc.ca/arctic/inuit/people.htm). This site has lots of information about the Inuit and links to other topics related to the Inuit. Also includes links to illustrations of a kayak, an igloo, and dogsleds.

Inuit 3D, Civilization.ca, Canadian Museum of Civilization (www.civilization.ca/aborig/inuit3d/vmc inuit_e.html). A virtual tour of the Inuit 3D Museum. This interesting site requires downloading software to view. May require adult supervision.

Index

Picture Credits

Cover image: © Hulton-Deutsch Collection/CORBIS
AP/Wide World Photos, 34, 37
© Bettmann/CORBIS, 12, 20
© CORBIS, 7
© Corel Corporation, 38
© Historical Society of Seattle & King County Museum of History/CORBIS, 9
© Hulton/Archive by Getty Images, 16–17, 24, 25, 31
© Hulton-Deutsch Collection/CORBIS, 11
© Lane Kennedy/CORBIS, 15
Library of Congress, 18, 21
© Michael Maslan Historic Photographs/CORBIS, 26–27
Time Life Pictures by Getty Images, 32
Werner Forman/Art Resource, NY, 28, 29

About the Authors

Charles George taught high school history and Spanish, and Linda George taught various grades on the elementary level in the Texas public schools before retiring to the mountains of New Mexico. Married for thirty-three years, Charles and Linda have written more than fifty young adult and children's nonfiction books. Charles wrote *The Comanche* and *The Sioux* for the North American Indians series. He and Linda wrote *Texas* for the Seeds of a Nation series and *The Maya* for the Blackbirch series Life During the Great Civilizations.